JUST A BITE

JUST A BITE

POLLY TYRER

PRENTICE
HALL
PRESS

New York London Toronto Sydney Tokyo Singapore

Prentice Hall Press
15 Columbus Circle
New York, New York 10023

Produced, designed and edited by Shuckburgh Reynolds Ltd.

Published in Great Britain by Macdonald & Co (Publishers) Ltd.
Design by Clare Clements
Photography by Martin Brigdale
Home Economy by Polly Tyrer

PRENTICE HALL PRESS and colophon are registered trademarks of Simon & Schuster Inc.

Library of Congress Cataloging-in-Publication Data
Tyrer, Polly
   Just a bite.

   Includes index.
   1. Cookery (Appetizers)   2. Snack foods.
3. Entertaining.   I. Title
TX740.T97   1986   641.8'12   86-12322
ISBN 0-13-514076-5

Filmset by SX Composing Ltd, Rayleigh.
Printed in Portugal by Printer Portuguesa
10 9 8 7 6 5 4 3

ACKNOWLEDGEMENTS

Thanks to Gila Falkus for her painstaking work editing this book; to Jenny Kieldsen for help with the home economy and generally getting things right; to Leith's Good Food Ltd, especially Anne Renowden and Robert Kelso; to Prue Leith and Cynthia Vivian for the loan of their cookery libraries; and, for general help and good ideas, to Seemah Joshua, Annie Langford and those at Springfield Farm.

CONTENTS

INTRODUCTION

In the 1920s and 30s cocktail parties with their dry martinis, canapés and ladies in elegant black dresses, were considered the height of style. Then, for over forty years, the idea of a cocktail party became as stale as the dried up nibbles that were usually served. But today, cocktail parties are once again in vogue, hard on the heels of glamorous cocktail lounges. Gone is the austere image — cocktails are bright and exotic, and cocktail food is fresh and imaginative.

It is hardly surprising that the cocktail party has survived – they certainly have much to recommend them. You can pay back all those dinner party invitations at one time. The menu can be adapted for weddings, christenings, birthdays, "just drinks", or even barbecues. You can also have a lot of fun creating delicious-tasting and irresistible-looking food. The only rules to remember are that it must be small enough to eat in one or two bites and not too messy to be picked up with the fingers. But although most people know how to cook a meal for their family and friends, they have no idea how to prepare cocktail food for a party of 50. This book gives lots of new recipe ideas and also some advice on how to estimate quantities and how to tackle the problems that you may encounter. Recipes range from the ultra-sophisticated to the casual and some menu suggestions for various different occasions are given on pages 152 and 153.

Each recipe in this book will make about 20 mouthfuls of food. For a cocktail party you should allow 10 mouthfuls of food per head; 4 mouthfuls with pre-lunch or dinner drinks; for a wedding reception 8 spicy plus 4 sweet mouthfuls (but increase this to 15 mouthfuls if the guests are unlikely to go for a meal afterwards).

Bear in mind how the food will be prepared and carefully select the menu so that there is not too much work to do on the day of the party. Some items freeze well; some are quick to make; some need last-minute attention. The recipes indicate how much preparation can be done in advance. Don't leave too many things to be done after the guests arrive or you will be a slave at your own party.

As a general rule, choose food that will offer a variety of texture, color and flavor and think about its presentation. Cold cocktail nibbles can be arranged as an assortment on a platter. This is best done in tightly packed rows decorated with watercress and olives or radish slices. Food accompanied by a dip can be served on a round plate with the dip in the center. Hot nibbles are best served with only one variety on each plate.

Make a shopping list well in advance and be prepared to spend some time doing this thoroughly. Check the availability of any unusual ingredients – hunting around at the last minute can be irritatingly time consuming. Suppliers tend to be keen to let you know that most foods are available all year round, but when it comes to the crunch, there can be some obscure reason why they haven't, after all, got what you require. "Spinach only arrives on Tuesdays," "Crab claws are scarce in spring because the crabs are not yet large enough to harvest", and so on. Pin your supplier down and give your order well in advance. It is far better to change the menu sooner than later if there is any doubt about availability.

When it comes to preparation, the most speedy method of tackling cocktail party food is undoubtedly by a production line method. For example, Smoked Salmon Wheels (p. 45) are best made in the following stages:

1. Lay out all the bread slices in pairs.
2. Flatten them all with a rolling pin.
3. Butter all the bread.
4. Cover the bread with smoked salmon.
5. Season with lemon juice and black pepper.
6. Roll up and chill in the refrigerator.
7. Slice all the rolls and trim them neatly.

The choice of menu will also depend on whether waiters or waitresses will help serve on the day of the party. If there is to be no help at all, it is best to limit the choice of food to 5 items and not to include more than 2 hot choices. (That is, if allowing 10 mouthfuls of food per guest, choose 5 different items and make 2 of each kind for each person.) If you are employing help, allow one server for every 35 guests for the food, one bartender for every 50 guests if only serving a limited selection of drinks (e.g., sherry, wine and a soft drink), and one bartender per 30 guests if serving mixed drinks or cocktails.

Deciding on how much drink to supply can be a tricky question. It is disastrous for a cocktail party to run dry and as most liquor stores supply on a sale or return basis, it is best to over-order. Remember, though, that any bottles left over must be returned completely intact, including the labels.

There are many options as to how much variety of drink to supply. It is perfectly acceptable to offer only wine or champagne. A small bar of perhaps wine, one or two kinds of liquor and sherry is another alternative, or a full bar with even a choice of two or three cocktails, if you are really ambitious. The budget will probably be the deciding factor. Whatever you decide, always include some mineral water and fruit juice for the non-drinkers, drivers and those just trying to sober up before going home.

The drinks can be served either from a tended bar or wine and a small selection can be passed around on trays. One bottle of wine holds 6 glasses. If only wine or champagne are being served, allow half a bottle per person. When buying wine, two-thirds should be white and one-third red. For mixed drinks, in my experience, vodka and Scotch are the most popular liquors with gin and rum coming close second. Campari, dry and sweet vermouth and sherry should also be available. For a mixed bar for 50 people a reasonable order would consist of:

Vodka, 3 bottles	**White Wine**, 9 bottles
Scotch, 3 bottles	**Red Wine**, 4 bottles
Gin, 1 bottle	**Club Soda**, 24 small bottles
Dry Vermouth, 1 bottle	**Tonic**, 24 small bottles
Sweet Vermouth, 1 bottle	**Ginger Ale**, 12 small bottles
Campari, 1 bottle	**Tomato Juice**, 3 quarts
Dubonnet, 1 bottle	**Orange Juice**, 12 quarts
Dry Sherry, 2 bottles	**Bitter Lemon**, 12 small bottles
Sweet Sherry, 1 bottle	**Cola**, 12 cans
Brandy, ½ bottle	**Mineral Water**, 12 quarts

There are many books available containing recipes and suggestions for cocktails. Unless you really want to go to town, a choice of three cocktails should be enough. Look closely at the list of ingredients before you start: some recipes require a dash of this and a drop of something else and suddenly the whole exercise can become quite expensive. Remember also, that unless you have "help", you can easily become a slave at your own party.

If there is not sufficient refrigerator space for cooling wine, allow 10 lb of ice for each case. Place the bottles in a large plastic bowl (a baby's bath is ideal) and pour the ice on top. If ice is only needed for drinks, make a few extra trays and store the cubes in a plastic bag in the freezer. Crushed ice for cocktails can be made in a blender or food processor at the last minute.

For a cocktail party to be enjoyable, it is important to keep the number of guests manageable. It is all too easy for an overcrowded room to feel like a zoo. As a rough guide, two average-sized rooms (or one large living room) will be comfortable for 50 people. But remember to count helpers when adding up the numbers and don't forget to allow space for your bar. The type of party will indicate the space and facilities needed. For instance, a wedding reception is likely to involve a few older people and to last longer than an evening cocktail party, so provision should be made for a few small tables and chairs.

It is a good idea to rehearse the party in your mind to check whether you have everything you need. Where will the coats go? Have you enough plates? Can all the food be eaten with fingers only? Will you need napkins? What about ashtrays? glasses? coasters? Liquor stores

13

will usually supply glasses free of charge if they are providing the drink. If you need more than glasses, there are many party equipment rental companies (see the Rental Checklist opposite).

For a formal cocktail party, it is usual to send a written or printed invitation and this should state what time the guests are expected to leave as well as to arrive. The idea is to give guests the opportunity to make arrangements for a meal afterwards, but it can also be useful to the host in preventing the party from lasting all evening. It is usually sensible, though, to assume that there will be a few hangers on and to have some more substantial food available (in your freezer, for instance) in case they would like to stay for dinner. For a more casual party, a telephone call to the guests is all that is necessary. If the time the party should end is important, let them know then – tactfully.

A cocktail party is an ideal way to entertain. It can be anything you like – extravagant, economical, small and sophisticated or a really large "bash". With careful planning and by following these guidelines, the host or hostess can prepare the food, be free to enjoy themselves and be remembered for giving a cocktail party with a difference.

Rental Check List

CHINA
6-inch plates for guests to put
  food on
10-inch plates for serving hot
  food and food with dips
Small bowls for serving dips

GLASSWARE
(allow 1½ glasses per guest)
Sherry glasses
Brandy snifters
Tulip-champagne and white wine
  glasses
Whisky tumblers for mixed drinks
  and soft drinks
Tall tumblers for cocktails and
  soft drinks
Goblets for red wine and mixed
  drinks
Water pitchers for fruit juice

TABLEWARE
Oval serving dishes
Round serving dishes
Ice bowls and spoons
Serving trays for passing drinks
Tablecloths to cover bar, serving
  tables and any small tables
  used
Ashtrays
Linen napkins for service
Paper napkins (small cocktail size
  ones are very handy)
Tea cloths
Plastic ice buckets or baby's bath
Trestle tables for bar and food
Card tables, if needed, round the
  room
Chairs
Coat rail, hangers, tickets and
  pins

FISH

Top: *Smoked Halibut on Rye with Salmon Roe and Lime;* right: *Smoked Trout Mousse and Smoked Salmon Parcels;* bottom: *Spinach Roulade with Smoked Salmon Mousse and Taramasalata Toasties;* center: *New Potatoes with Sour Cream and Mock Caviar and a Cream Puff with Curried Crab and Apple.*

FRITTO MISTO WITH GREEN MAYONNAISE

¼ lb squid, cleaned
¼ lb sole, whiting or flounder fillets
¼ lb raw jumbo shrimp
¼ lb bay scallops
Oil for deep-frying
Seasoned flour
FOR THE BATTER
½ cup all-purpose flour
Pinch of salt
1 egg, separated
⅓ cup each milk and water, mixed
2 tsp oil
FOR THE SAUCE
1 bunch watercress
1¼ cups mayonnaise

First make the sauce: Wash the watercress thoroughly in salted water and remove the stalks. Purée with 1 tbsp of boiling water. Stir into the mayonnaise and set aside in a small round dish.

Cut the squid into rings, the white fish into strips and the shrimp in half.

Remove the tough muscles opposite the corals from the scallops.

TO MAKE THE BATTER: Sift the flour and salt into a bowl, make a well in the center and drop in the egg yolk. mix, gradually adding the milk and water and incorporating the flour from the sides, until smooth and creamy. Add the oil. Beat the egg white until stiff and fold into the mixture.

Heat the oil for frying until a drop of batter will sizzle slowly. Dust the fish with seasoned flour, dip in the batter and fry, a few pieces at a time, until golden-brown. Drain on paper towels and sprinkle with salt. Serve immediately on a plate with the green mayonnaise in the center.

SMOKED TROUT MOUSSE AND SMOKED SALMON PARCELS

1 large smoked trout
3 tbsp heavy cream, lightly whipped
Lemon juice
1 tsp horseradish sauce
Salt and freshly ground black pepper
6 oz smoked salmon
20 tiny sprigs of dill

Cut the head and tail off the smoked trout and remove the skin and bones. Grind the flesh or chop it in a food processor. Mix with the whipped cream and season with the lemon juice, horseradish, salt and pepper. Cut the smoked salmon into 40 strips, roughly 1 inch×3 inches. Lay two strips of smoked salmon on the work surface, arranged in a cross. Put a spoonful of smoked trout mousse in the center of the cross and fold the ends over the top. Decorate with dill.

TIP: The smoked trout mousse freezes well. The parcels can be made the day before and stored in the refrigerator, covered in plastic wrap.

CREAM PUFFS WITH CURRIED CRAB AND APPLE

20 cream puffs (see recipe, p.146)
6 oz white king crabmeat, frozen or canned
½ red apple, grated with the skin on
⅔ cup mayonnaise
Curry paste
Milk
Paprika

Defrost the frozen crabmeat slowly. Drain well and pat dry with paper towels. Mix with the grated apple. Flavor the mayonnaise with enough curry paste to give a mild, spicy flavor. (If the mayonnaise is very thick, thin it to a coating consistency with a little milk.) Mix the crab and apple with the mayonnaise. Slit the cream puffs halfway through with a diagonal cut from top to bottom. Fill with the crab mixture and sprinkle with paprika.

SCALLOP MOUSSELINES

2 large sea scallops
6 oz raw haddock fillet, skin removed
1 egg white
⅔ cup heavy cream, chilled
Parsley, finely minced
Salt and ground white pepper
Anchovy paste
Lemon juice
20 puff pastry croûtes (see recipe p. 150)
1 tbsp mayonnaise
1 tbsp fresh herbs, finely minced

Remove the corals and tough muscles (opposite the corals) from the scallops. Discard the muscles. Plunge the corals into boiling water, then immediately into cold water. Drain and cut into ¼-inch pieces and set aside. Pat the scallops very dry with paper towels. Purée with the haddock and egg white in a blender or food processor. Turn into a bowl, cover and chill for several hours. Lightly whip 2 tbsp cream, gradually beat the rest into the scallop mixture. Fold in the whipped cream. Add the chopped corals, parsley and season with salt, pepper, anchovy paste and lemon juice. Butter two sheets of aluminum foil. Spoon the scallop mixture in lines about 2 inches away from the narrow edge of each sheet. Carefully roll up into a sausage with the foil and twist the ends to tighten.

Preheat the oven to 350°F. Fill a roasting pan with 2 inches of boiling water. Place the mousselines in the roasting pan and bake for about 20 minutes. Unwrap one mousseline to check that it feels quite firm. If not, continue to bake for a few minutes more. Chill overnight. Mix the mayonnaise with the fresh herbs. Unroll the scallop mousselines and cut into slices. Spread each puff pastry croûte with a little herb mayonnaise and top with a slice of mousseline.

JUMBO SHRIMP WITH SNOW PEAS

20 jumbo shrimp
3 tbsp peanut oil
1 tbsp lemon juice
1 clove garlic, crushed
Salt and freshly ground black pepper
1 tsp chopped mint
10 fresh snow peas

Peel the shrimp and place them in a dish. Pour over the oil, lemon juice, garlic, salt and pepper. Leave to marinate for about 6 hours. Add the chopped mint. Top and tail the snow peas. Plunge them into boiling water for 3 minutes, then immediately into cold water. Drain and pat dry on paper towels. Split the snow peas in half along the seams. Wrap in a spiral around each shrimp and skewer with a cocktail toothpick.

MUSSELS IN THEIR SHELLS WITH GARLIC BUTTER

20 mussels
1¼ cups water
½ onion, sliced, a few sprigs of parsley, 1 bay leaf
4 tbsp butter
2 cloves garlic, crushed
1 tbsp parsley, minced
Salt and freshly ground black pepper
1 tbsp bread crumbs
1 tbsp finely grated Gruyère cheese

Tap the mussels on the work surface and discard any that remain open. Scrub the rest and put them in a large pan with the water, onion, parsley sprigs and bay leaf. Cover and simmer for 2 minutes, shaking the pan occasionally until the mussels have opened. Strain and discard any mussels which remain closed. Remove the top half of each shell. Soften the butter and beat in the garlic and parsley and season with salt and pepper. Mix the bread crumbs and cheese together. Just before serving, preheat the broiler. Put a dab of garlic butter on each mussel and sprinkle with the topping. Broil until browned.

HERB-COATED KNOTS OF FLOUNDER WITH SAFFRON DIP

1 whole flounder, filleted
1 egg, beaten
Salt
Milk
Dry white bread crumbs
1 heaping tbsp minced mixed fresh herbs
Seasoned flour
Oil for deep-frying
FOR THE SAFFRON DIP
⅔ cup fish stock
4 strands saffron
⅔ cup thick mayonnaise
Salt and freshly ground black pepper
Pinch of ground turmeric
Squeeze of lemon juice

Cut the flounder fillets into thin strips, roughly ¼ inch × 4 inches, and tie them into knots. Mix the beaten egg with a pinch of salt and a little milk. Mix the breadcrumbs and herbs together. Dip the knots of flounder first into the seasoned flour, then into the egg and milk and finally into the bread crumbs. Make sure they are evenly coated.

TO MAKE THE SAFFRON DIP: Boil the fish stock until reduced to 1 tbsp. Soak the saffron strands in the hot stock. Leave to cool. Strain the stock and mix it with the mayonnaise. Season with salt, pepper, turmeric and lemon juice. Place in a small dish. Heat the oil until a cube of bread dropped in will sizzle vigorously. Fry the flounder until golden-brown. Drain on paper towels and sprinkle with salt. Serve immediately on a round plate with the saffron dip in the center, or leave to cool and reheat for 10 minutes in an oven preheated to 375°F just before serving.

TIP: The knots of flounder can be coated with egg and bread crumbs the day before, covered with plastic wrap and stored in the refrigerator overnight. Sole can be used instead of flounder if preferred.

MINI ARNOLD BENNETT OMELETS

3 eggs, separated
1 tbsp heavy cream
1 tbsp grated Parmesan cheese
Freshly ground black pepper
¼ lb smoked haddock, cooked
2 tbsp whipped cream
1 tomato, skinned and deseeded
Cayenne pepper and 1 tsp lemon juice

Preheat the oven to 375°F. Line a jelly roll pan roughly 8 inches x 12 inches with greased parchment paper. Mix the egg yolks with the cream and Parmesan cheese. Beat the egg whites until stiff and fold into the yolks. Season with pepper. Turn into the pan and bake for 10-12 minutes. Leave to cool. Chop the haddock very finely, stir in the whipped cream and chopped tomato, season with lemon juice and black and cayenne peppers.

Turn the cold omelet on to a sheet of parchment paper. Peel off the lining paper and spread with the smoked haddock mixture. Roll up like a tiny jelly roll. Trim the untidy edges and cut into about 20 slices.

SMOKED HALIBUT ON RYE WITH SALMON ROE AND LIME

10 slices light rye bread
Butter for spreading
6 oz smoked halibut
1 lime
Freshly ground black pepper
2 oz salmon roe

Cut two 2-inch circles from each slice of bread and spread with butter. Cut circles of smoked halibut and lay on top of the buttered bread. With a vegetable or citrus peeler, remove thin strips of rind from the lime, taking care not to remove any of the pith. With a sharp knife, cut the rind into the finest shreds. Plunge into boiling water, then immediately into cold water. Squeeze the juice from the lime, grind a little black pepper into it, and brush over the smoked halibut. Place a small mound of salmon roe on top of each canapé. Garnish with shreds of lime.
TIP: Smoked halibut can be bought sliced, like smoked salmon, from most good delicatessens.

SPINACH ROULADE FILLED WITH SMOKED SALMON MOUSSE

4 oz frozen chopped spinach
1 tbsp butter
2 eggs, separated
Salt and freshly ground black pepper
Ground nutmeg
½ lb smoked salmon pieces
Milk
2 tsp mayonnaise
2 tsp whipped cream
Lemon juice

Preheat the oven to 375°F. Defrost the spinach. Line a jelly roll pan roughly 8 inches × 12 inches with greased parchment paper. Melt the butter, add the spinach and stir over high heat until the excess moisture has evaporated. Cool a little, add the egg yolks and season with salt, pepper and nutmeg. Beat the egg whites until stiff and fold into the spinach mixture. Turn into the pan and bake for 10-12 minutes. Leave to cool.

Purée the smoked salmon in a blender or food processor, adding a little milk to make a thick paste. Stir in the mayonnaise and cream and season with lemon juice and pepper.

Lay a sheet of parchment paper on the work surface and turn the cold roulade on to it. Peel off the lining paper and cut the roulade in half crosswise. Spread the smoked salmon mousse over each half and roll up like tiny jelly rolls. Trim the untidy edges and cut each roulade into 10 slices.

BROILED CLAMS WITH PROVENÇALE TOPPING

20 littleneck clams
6 tbsp butter
1 shallot, minced
1 canned tomato, finely chopped
1 clove garlic, crushed
1 tbsp bread crumbs
Chopped parsley

Make sure that the clams are still alive by tapping the shells. Discard any that remain open. Push the sharp edge of a knife blade firmly between the shells, opposite the hinge. Twist the knife to open the clams and remove the top shell from each one. Preheat the broiler. Soften the butter and beat in the shallot, tomato, garlic and bread crumbs. Put a spoonful of the topping on each clam and broil for a few minutes, until the topping is lightly browned and the clams are cooked. Decorate with chopped parsley.

Shrimp Puffs

1 recipe quantity savory cream puff pastry (see
    p.146)
¼ lb shrimp, cooked and peeled
¼ cup finely diced Cheddar cheese
¼ cup oil for deep-frying
2 tbsp grated Parmesan cheese

Mix the shrimp and diced cheese into the cream puff pastry. Heat the oil until a small piece of the paste dropped in will sizzle vigorously. Use 2 teaspoons to shape the mixture into even-sized balls and drop them into the hot oil (making sure each one has shrimp inside it). Fry a few at a time until puffed up and golden-brown. Drain on paper towels and then sprinkle with Parmesan cheese. Serve immediately, and hand cocktail toothpicks and napkins separately.

DILL BLINIS WITH SOUR CREAM AND GRAVLAX

¼ lb salmon fillet, in one piece, unskinned
1 tsp olive oil
1 tsp chopped fresh dill
1 tsp salt and ½ tsp superfine sugar
½ tsp crushed green peppercorns
⅔ cup sour cream
FOR THE BLINIS
½ cup each all-purpose and wholewheat
   flour, mixed half and half
Pinch of salt
½ tsp baking soda and ½ tsp cream of tartar
1 egg, beaten
⅔ cup milk
1 tsp chopped dill

Lay the salmon skin-side down on a piece of aluminum foil. Rub with olive oil and sprinkle with the dill, salt, sugar and peppercorns. Wrap up tightly and chill for 24 hours, turning twice.

TO MAKE THE BLINIS: Sift the flour, salt, baking soda and cream of tartar together into a mixing bowl. Make a well in the center, add the egg and beat. Stir in the milk until the batter is the consistency of lightly whipped cream. (It may not be necessary to add all the milk.) Add the dill and leave to stand for 10 minutes.

Grease a heavy skillet or griddle and heat it. When very hot, drop 2 or 3 small spoonfuls of batter on to the surface, keeping them well separated. When the underside is brown and bubbles have risen to the surface, turn the blinis to brown the other side. To serve the blinis: Wrap them in foil and warm in a moderate oven. Cut the gravlax into thin strips. Place a spoonful of sour cream in the middle of each blini and arrange the strips of gravlax on top in a lattice pattern.

NOTE: True blinis are made with a yeast batter but this is very time-consuming. The recipe above cheats a little to be speedy, but is delicious nonetheless. Blinis freeze well.

NEW POTATOES WITH SOUR CREAM AND MOCK CAVIAR

20 even-sized tiny new potatoes
Vinaigrette dressing
⅔ cup sour cream
1 small jar black lumpfish roe

Scrub the potatoes and cook in gently simmering salted water until tender, about 20 minutes. Drain and, while still hot, soak in the vinaigrette dressing until cool. Lift the potatoes out of the dressing and pat dry with paper towels. Cut a small slice from the bottom of each potato so that it can sit flat. Carefully scoop a hollow from the top with a melon-baller. Fill the hollows with a spoonful of sour cream and top with the lumpfish roe.

TIP: The potatoes can be boiled and soaked in vinaigrette dressing overnight.

SMOKED MUSSELS IN CHEESE PASTRY

4 oz canned smoked mussels
1 recipe quantity cheese pastry
*   (p.147)*
½ egg, beaten

Drain the smoked mussels and lay on paper towels to dry. Roll the pastry out thinly and stamp out 2-inch circles with a plain pastry cutter. Place a smoked mussel in the center of each one. Brush the edges with the beaten egg and fold over like a tiny turnover. Seal the edges together with a fork or knife, marking a pattern on the pastry at the same time. Chill. Just before serving, preheat the oven to 400°F, brush the pastry with beaten egg and bake for 10-15 minutes. Or bake ahead of time and serve cold, but do not reheat.

MARINATED HALIBUT AND SALMON PINWHEELS

¼ lb salmon fillet, skinned, in one piece
¼ lb halibut fillet, skinned, in one piece
Juice of ½ lemon
1 tbsp white wine
1 tbsp superfine sugar
1 tbsp finely chopped fresh tarragon or 1 tsp dried
¼ lb fresh spinach
⅔ cup mayonnaise
Salt and freshly ground black pepper
20 puff pastry croûtes (see recipe p.150)

With a very sharp knife, slice the salmon and halibut fillets in half horizontally to make four very thin fillets. Place them between two layers of plastic wrap and flatten them with the back of a knife. Marinate the salmon in the lemon juice, white wine, sugar and half the tarragon for about 4 hours. Add the halibut and marinate for an additional 2 hours. Wash the spinach and remove the tough stalks. Plunge it first into boiling salted water and then into cold water. Lay the leaves out flat on a clean tea towel. Drain and pat the fish dry with paper towels. Place the two fillets on the work surface, cover with spinach leaves and put the plaice on top. Roll up like jelly rolls, wrap tightly in aluminum foil and refrigerate for at least 1 hour.

To assemble the pinwheels: Cut the rolls of fish into thin slices. Mix the remaining tarragon with the mayonnaise and season with salt and pepper. Spread each circle of puff pastry with some mayonnaise and top with a salmon and halibut pinwheel.

TIP: Ask the fishmarket for long flat fillets rather than thick steaks.

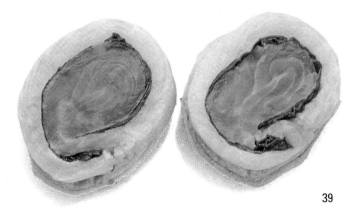

SEVICHE SKEWERED WITH COCKTAIL AVOCADO

5 sea scallops
6 oz salmon or pink trout
Juice of 1 lime
1 shallot, minced
2 tbsp olive oil
½ red chili pepper, minced
2 ripe cocktail avocados

Wash the scallops and remove the tough muscles (opposite the coral). Cut into quarters. Skin the salmon or pink trout and remove any bones. Cut into bite-sized pieces. Put the fish in a dish and pour on the lime juice, shallot and oil. Cover tightly with plastic wrap and chill overnight. Not more than 1 hour before serving, add the red chili pepper to the seviche and marinate for a an extra 15 minutes. Meanwhile peel the avocados, cut in half lengthwise and then into chunks. Drain the seviche and pat dry on paper towels. Turn the avocados in the marinade to prevent them from going brown. Thread on to cocktail toothpicks with the avocado sandwiched between a piece of salmon and a piece of scallop.

TARAMASALATA TOASTIES

½ slice white bread, crusts removed
1 clove garlic, crushed
4 oz smoked cod roe, skinned
⅔ cup salad oil
Lemon juice
Freshly ground black pepper
20 slivers of black olive
20 toastie cases (see recipe p. 148)

Soak the bread in cold water and squeeze dry. Place it in a bowl with the crushed garlic and cod roe. With a wooden spoon or electric beater, gradually beat the oil in, drop by drop. (Alternatively, put the bread, garlic and cod roe into a food processor and gradually add the oil.) Season with lemon juice and pepper. Put the taramasalata into a pastry bag fitted with a fluted tip and pipe in whirls into the toastie cases. Garnish with a sliver of black olive.

TIP: The taramasalata will keep in the refrigerator for up to a week.

MUSHROOM AND OYSTER BOUCHÉES

2 tbsp butter
Salt and freshly ground black pepper
¼ lb flat black mushrooms, minced
1 shallot, minced
20 baked patty shells (see recipe p.149)
8 oz canned smoked oysters
FOR THE LEMON HOLLANDAISE
1 egg yolk
4 tbsp butter
1 tbsp lemon juice
Salt and freshly ground black pepper

Melt 2 tbsp of butter in a skillet, add the mushrooms and shallots and cook gently until soft. Season with salt and pepper.
TO MAKE THE LEMON HOLLANDAISE: Place the egg yolk in a small bowl with a pinch of salt and a knob of the butter. Set over a pan of barely simmering water. Stir the mixture until slightly thickened and gradually beat in the remaining butter and lemon juice, allowing the sauce to thicken each time before adding more. Season with pepper.

Put a spoonful of the mushroom mixture in the base of each patty shell. Pop an oyster (or half an oyster if they are too large) into each patty shell on top of the mushroom mixture. Preheat the broiler. Top each shell with a dollop of lemon hollandaise and broil until lightly browned. Serve immediately.

TIP: Fresh oysters can be used instead of smoked. Ask the fish market to open them but be sure to use them the same day. Fry the fresh oysters briskly in a little butter just before adding to the patty shells.

LOBSTER MOUSSE IN PASTRY CASES

1 recipe quantity cheese pastry (see recipe
    p.147)
½ lb cooked lobster meat
2 tbsp mayonnaise
2 tbsp heavy cream, whipped
Salt, freshly ground black pepper and
    Tabasco sauce
Lemon juice
1 envelope unflavored gelatin
Paprika

Roll the pastry thinly and stamp out 2-inch circles with a plain pastry cutter. Press into mini muffin pans and chill for 30 minutes. Preheat the oven to 400°F. Fill each pastry shell with a crumpled piece of aluminum foil and bake for 10-15 minutes. Cool. Purée the lobster meat with the mayonnaise. Fold in the cream. Season with salt, pepper, Tabasco sauce and lemon juice. Put a spoonful of water into a pan and sprinkle in the gelatin. Soak for 10 minutes, then warm gently until clear and runny. Add to the lobster and mix well. Pipe into the pastry shells.

SMOKED SALMON WHEELS

8 slices brown bread, crusts removed
Butter for spreading
6 oz smoked salmon
Lemon juice
Freshly ground black pepper
Alfalfa sprouts, to garnish

Lay 2 slices of bread on the work surface with the edges overlapping by
½ inch. Flatten them with a rolling pin, making sure that the edges are
well-pressed together. Butter the bread and cover with smoked salmon. Brush with lemon juice and sprinkle with pepper. Roll up like a
jelly roll. Repeat with the remaining 6 slices. Pack tightly together in a
box covered with plastic wrap and chill for 30 minutes. Trim the untidy
edges from each smoked salmon roll and cut into five. Garnish with a
light sprinkling of the alfalfa sprouts.
TIP: The smoked salmon rolls can be frozen before they are sliced.
Wrap each roll individually in plastic wrap before freezing.

MEAT

Left to right: *Smoked Chicken Bites; Salami on Black Rye with Marinated Beets; Ham, Cream Cheese and Chive Pinwheels; Mini Antipasto; Steak Tartare.*

TOASTIES WITH PÂTÉ AND GREEN PEPPERCORNS

½ lb chicken or duck livers
1 stick (4 oz) butter
1 medium-sized onion, minced
1 clove garlic, crushed
Salt and freshly ground black pepper
2 tbsp plain yogurt
2 ½-oz jar green peppercorns
20 toastie cases (see recipe p.148)

Discard any discolored bits from the livers. Melt the butter in a heavy-based skillet, add the onion and garlic and cook gently until soft and transparent. Add the livers and cook, turning occasionally until they are brown all over and cooked right through. Season well with salt and pepper. Purée the pâté in a blender or food processor with the yogurt and a teaspoonful of green peppercorns. Put the pâté into a pastry bag fitted with a fluted tip and pipe into the toastie cases. Garnish each one with a green peppercorn.

TIP: The pâté can be kept in the refrigerator for up to 3 days. It also freezes well.

RUMAKI

10 slices bacon
¼ lb chicken livers
1 tsp brown sugar
1 tbsp hot water
1 tbsp soy sauce
Pinch of five spice powder
1 clove garlic, crushed
Pinch of salt
20 slices of water chestnuts

Stretch the bacon with the back of a knife and cut each slice in half. Discard any discolored bits from the livers and cut into bite-sized pieces. Dissolve the brown sugar in the hot water and add the soy sauce, five spice powder, garlic and salt. Add the chicken livers and leave to marinate for 2-4 hours. Preheat the oven to 425°F. Drain the livers well. Place each piece of liver with a slice of water chestnut and wrap in a strip of bacon. Set on a baking sheet with the seam underneath and bake the rumaki for 10 minutes until golden-brown. **TIP:** Rumaki can be made the day before and chilled overnight.

RED LETTUCE WITH SALADE TIÈDE

20 red lettuce leaves
2-3 curly endive leaves
¼ lb chicken livers
1 tbsp walnut oil
2 slices bacon, diced
⅔ cup sliced button mushrooms

Wash and dry the lettuce leaves. Wash, dry and chop the curly endive. Discard any discolored bits from the liver and cut into small thin slices. Just before serving, heat the oil in a heavy skillet. When hot, add the sliced liver and bacon and cook briskly until well-browned on all sides. Add the mushrooms and cook for another minute. Add this mixture, including any liquid in the pan, to the chopped endive. Season with salt and pepper and toss well. Tuck a little of the mixture inside each lettuce leaf and secure with a cocktail toothpick.

TIP: This recipe must be made and served at the last minute. The livers will be dry and tough if reheated and the lettuce leaves soon wilt once they are filled with the warm salad. It is therefore not suitable for parties of more than 20 people.

PORK AND SHRIMP TOASTS

6 oz ground pork
⅓ cup finely chopped, cooked, peeled shrimp
1 tbsp finely chopped cilantro leaves
1 clove garlic, crushed
1 tsp anchovy paste
½ small egg, beaten
Salt and freshly ground black pepper
3 slices stale bread, crusts removed
Oil for deep-frying
Extra sprigs of cilantro for garnish

Place the pork and shrimp, cilantro, garlic, anchovy paste and beaten egg together in a bowl and season well with salt and pepper. Knead and squeeze the mixture together until it has a pasty consistency. Spread the pork and shrimp mixture thickly on the bread. Cut each slice into eight triangles. Heat the oil until a piece of bread dropped in will sizzle vigorously. Fry a few triangles at a time, meat-side down, until crisp and brown. Drain well on paper towels and keep warm while the remaining toasts are cooking. It is important to allow the oil to regain heat each time or the toasts will be greasy and soggy.
Serve immediately, garnished with sprigs of cilantro.

VENISON SAUSAGES WITH CRANBERRY SAUCE

6 oz ground pork
3 oz ground veal
3 oz ground venison
Bread crumbs to coat
1 tsp ground allspice
½ tsp dried sage
Salt and freshly ground black pepper
A little flour
Pork fat
Cranberry sauce

Mix the ground meats together and add the bread crumbs, allspice and sage and season with salt and pepper. With floured hands, shape the mixture into little sausages about 2 inches long. Dust with flour. Put the pork fat in a roasting pan and melt over moderate heat on top of the stove. When hot, add the sausages and brown on all sides. Turn the heat down and continue to fry, turning occasionally until cooked all the way through. Serve on cocktail toothpicks on a round plate with cranberry sauce in the center.

MINI BARBECUE RIBLETS

1 lb pork spareribs
1 tbsp clear honey
1 tbsp soy sauce
2 tbsp orange juice
⅔ cup tomato catsup
1 clove garlic, crushed
Salt and freshly ground black pepper

With a sharp knife, scrape away ¼ inch of meat from one end of each riblet to expose a little bone (so that they can be held easily with the fingers). Mix all the rest of the ingredients together. Put the riblets into a shallow container, pour the marinade over, cover and chill overnight. The following day, preheat the oven to 375°F. Place the riblets with the marinade into a roasting pan and bake for about 1 hour until the ribs are very tender and the marinade has reduced to a dark sticky glaze. Alternatively, drain the riblets and grill them over a not-too-fierce barbecue.

TIP: Ask the butcher to cut the ribs apart and then into 2-inch lengths. If he cannot be persuaded to do this, the job can be accomplished with a sharp knife and a cleaver. But do take care.

SALAMI WITH MARINATED BEETS ON PUMPERNICKEL

¼ lb raw beets
2 tbsp vinaigrette dressing
1 tsp wholegrain mustard
Pinch cumin seeds
10 slices pumpernickel bread
Butter for spreading
¼ lb salami, about 1½ inches in diameter

Cut the beets into thin slices. Stamp out small fluted circles with a decorative pastry cutter. Mix the vinaigrette dressing with the mustard and cumin seeds. Place the beets in a dish, pour the dressing over and leave to marinate for several hours.

Cut the pumpernickel bread into 1½-inch circles with a plain cutter and spread with butter. Slice the salami quite thickly and set a slice on top of each bread round. Drain the beets well, pat dry with paper towels and use to garnish the salami.

STEAK TARTARE

¼ lb filet mignon or rump steak
1 tbsp oil
1 raw egg yolk
½ small onion, minced
1 tsp minced parsley
Salt and freshly ground black pepper
Worcestershire sauce
20 dried white bread croûtes (see recipe,
    p.150)
1 hard-cooked egg or 20 capers

Trim the steak and chop or grind it two or three times until it is very
smooth. Beat in the oil, egg yolk, onion and parsley and season with
salt, pepper and Worcestershire sauce. Put a spoonful of steak tartare
on top of each bread croûte and garnish with sieved hard-cooked egg
yolk and chopped white, or with a caper.

TANDOORI CHICKEN WITH CUCUMBER AND YOGURT DIP

½ lb boneless chicken
⅔ cup plain yogurt
Pinch of chili, cumin and ground coriander
1 tsp garam masala
1 tsp tomato paste
Juice and grated rind of ½ lemon
1 clove garlic, crushed
1 tsp fresh ginger root, pared and chopped
Salt and freshly ground black pepper
FOR THE CUCUMBER AND YOGURT DIP
½ cucumber
⅔ cup plain yogurt
1 tbsp heavy cream
1 tbsp finely chopped fresh mint
Salt and freshly ground black pepper

Cut the chicken into bite-sized chunks. Place all the remaining ingredients together in a blender or food processor and purée until smooth. Lay the pieces of chicken in a shallow dish, pour the marinade over, cover and chill overnight.

The following day, just before serving, lift the chicken out of the marinade and place in a roasting pan. Preheat the broiler or oven to the highest temperature. Cook the chicken for about 10 minutes, until reddish-brown and tender. Spear with cocktail toothpicks and serve on a round dish surrounding the cucumber and yogurt dip.

CUCUMBER AND YOGURT DIP: Chop the cucumber finely and pat dry with paper towels to get rid of any excess moisture. Mix all the ingredients together and season with salt and pepper.

KOFTA KABOBS

½ lb lean lamb
½ tsp ground coriander
½ tsp ground cumin
2 tsp chopped fresh mint
2 tsp chopped cilantro or parsley
Mint leaves for garnish

Finely chop or grind the lamb and mix it thoroughly with all the seasonings. Shape into tiny oval nuggets and thread on to cocktail toothpicks, two nuggets on each one. Broil or barbecue for 10 minutes. Serve hot, garnished with the mint leaves.

MINI ANTIPASTO

3 large carrots
6 oz Boursin cheese
Milk
¼ green pepper, deseeded and chopped
¼ red pepper, deseeded and chopped
Salt and freshly ground black pepper
10 slices Mortadella sausage (cut as thinly as
    possible)

Pare the carrots. With the tip of a vegetable peeler, cut grooves the length of the carrot and all the way around. Cut each carrot into 8 pieces. Soften the Boursin with a little milk and mix with the chopped peppers. Season with salt and pepper. Cut the Mortadella into small circles, about 1 inch in diameter, with a plain pastry cutter.

Put a spoonful of the Boursin mixture on top of each piece of carrot. Make a cut in each circle of Mortadella from the outside to the center and arrange on top of the Boursin in a twist.

TIP: Most cooked sausages or salamis can be substituted for Mortadella in this recipe.

WAFER-THIN SLICES OF RAW BEEF WITH MUSTARD MAYONNAISE

½ lb filet mignon
5 slices cracked wheat bread, crusts removed
Butter for spreading
⅔ cup thick mayonnaise flavored with Dijon
mustard

Place the steak in the freezer until almost frozen. With a very sharp knife, cut the nearly frozen meat into wafer-thin slices. Place the slices of meat between two sheets of waxed paper and flatten them with a rolling pin.

Butter the bread and spread with a little mustard mayonnaise. Cover each slice with raw beef and cut into four triangles. Place the remaining mayonnaise in a pastry bag fitted with a small fluted tip and pipe a curl in the corner of each triangle.

TIP: Any lean, tender cut of beef can be used in this recipe but a neat result is most easily achieved with filet mignon.

PORK AND MANGO WITH SATÉ SAUCE

½ lb lean boneless pork
1 mango
FOR THE SATÉ SAUCE
2 tbsp crunchy peanut butter
½ small onion, minced
1 clove garlic, crushed
1 tsp fresh ginger root, pared and chopped
2 tsp brown sugar
Pinch chili powder and lemon grass
2 tbsp canned cream of coconut
⅔ cup boiling water

Cut the pork into bite-sized chunks. Pare the mango and cut the flesh into chunks about the same size as the pork. Make into little kabobs with a piece of pork and a piece of mango threaded on to a cocktail toothpick. Broil for about 10 minutes, turning halfway through cooking. Serve on a dish around the warm saté sauce.

TO MAKE THE SATÉ SAUCE: Combine all the ingredients in a pan and bring to a boil. Add a little extra water if the sauce is too thick.

SMOKED CHICKEN BITES

½ lb smoked boneless chicken, ground
1 stick (4 oz) butter, softened
1 tbsp snipped chives
1 tsp wholegrain mustard
Salt and freshly ground black pepper
5 tbsp toasted cracked wheat bread crumbs,
    crushed

Beat the chicken and butter together until smooth (or combine in a food processor). Add the snipped chives and mustard and season with salt and pepper. Shape into small balls and roll in the bread crumbs.
TIP: The smoked chicken mixture freezes well. The bites are also delicious served on cocktail toothpicks and dipped in mustard flavored mayonnaise or chili dip.

MINI CHEESE AND HAM CROISSANTS

8 oz puff pastry
¼ lb thinly sliced boiled ham
¼ lb Gruyère or Emmenthal cheese,
*   thinly sliced*
1 egg, beaten

Roll the puff pastry out thinly and cut it into ten 2-inch squares. Cut each square across and pull two points to form two elongated triangles from each square. Put a little ham and cheese in each one. Roll up the triangles from the longest edge towards the point and twist to form a croissant shape. Place on a damp baking sheet and chill for 30 minutes. Preheat the oven to 400°F. Brush with beaten egg and bake for 15-20 minutes, until well-risen, crisp and golden-brown.

TIP: The croissants can be filled and shaped the day before, tightly covered with plastic wrap and chilled overnight.

NUGGETS OF MARINATED LAMB

½ lb boneless lamb
⅔ cup peanut oil
1 tsp coriander seeds, crushed
1 tsp fennel seeds, crushed
1 tsp garam masala
Salt and freshly ground black pepper
½ lemon
Handful fresh rosemary

Trim the lamb and cut into ½-inch cubes. Mix all the marinade ingredients together except the lemon. Squeeze the juice from the lemon, then finely slice the rind and add both to the marinade. Mix the cubes of meat with the marinade, cover and chill overnight.

The following day, drain the cubes of lamb and thread onto cocktail toothpicks with two cubes of meat on each stick. Scatter over the fresh rosemary and broil or barbecue for 10 minutes, turning halfway through cooking and brushing with marinade. Serve hot.

TIP: This is also delicious served with saté sauce, p. 61.

HAM, CREAM CHEESE AND CHIVE PINWHEELS

8 slices brown bread, crusts removed
Butter for spreading
6 oz cream cheese
Milk
½ cup minced ham
1 tbsp snipped chives
Freshly ground black pepper
1 container alfalfa sprouts to garnish

Place two slices of bread on the work surface with the edges overlapping by ½ inch. Flatten them with a rolling pin, making sure that the edges are well-pressed together. Butter the bread. Repeat. Soften the cream cheese with a little milk and mix with the ham and chives and season with pepper. Spread a thick layer over the slices of bread. Roll up like a jelly roll. Pack tightly together in a box, cover with plastic wrap and chill for 30 minutes. Unwrap, trim the untidy edges and cut each roll into five slices. Serve lightly garnished with the alfalfa sprouts.

MOROCCAN LAMB PIES

½ lb cooked ground lamb
1 tbsp oil
1 stick (4 oz) butter
½ small onion, minced
½ tsp ground cumin
¼ cup slivered almonds
2 tsp honey
A handful of golden raisins
Salt and freshly ground black pepper
8 sheets of filo pastry

Melt 2 tbsp butter. Add the onion and cook gently until soft and transparent. Stir in the ground cumin and slivered almonds and continue to cook until the almonds are a little browned. Add the honey and golden raisins. Drain the mixture on paper towels and leave to cool. Mix with the ground lamb. Season with salt and pepper. Brush half the sheets of filo pastry with melted butter, cover with the remaining sheets and brush again with butter. Cut each pair of pastry sheets into five long strips. Place a spoonful of the lamb filling at one end of each strip of pastry. Form a triangle by folding the right hand corner to the opposite side, then fold over and then across from left to right. Continue folding until the strip of pastry is used.

Preheat the oven to 400°F. Place the lamb pies on a greased baking sheet. Brush the tops with melted butter and bake for about 10 minutes until golden-brown. Serve warm.

TIP: Prepared triangles keep in the refrigerator for up to two days or freeze them open on a tray, then wrap in plastic wrap until needed.

CHICKEN AND LOBSTER BOUCHÉES

½ lb cooked boneless chicken
¼ lb cooked lobster meat
⅔ cup mayonnaise
Milk or light cream
Salt and freshly ground black pepper
Lemon juice
Tabasco sauce
2 tbsp red lumpfish caviar
*20 baked patty shells (see recipe,
    p.149)*

Chop the chicken and lobster meat. Thin the mayonnaise with a little milk or cream to a coating consistency. Mix the mayonnaise with the chicken and lobster meat and season with salt, pepper, lemon juice and Tabasco sauce. Spoon into the patty shells and garnish with red lumpfish caviar.

MINI HAMBURGERS

¾ lb lean ground beef
1 tsp minced parsley
Salt and freshly ground black pepper
20 dried white bread croûtes (see recipe,
    p.150)
Mayonnaise flavored with Dijon mustard
2 dill pickles, finely sliced
Tomato-chili relish
3 small tomatoes, finely sliced
2 scallions, cut into strips

Mix the ground beef with the parsley and season with salt and pepper.
Shape into tiny hamburger-shaped patties about 1½ inches in diameter. Broil for 3 minutes a side, until dark brown on the outside and
still a little juicy in the middle. (This can be done on a barbecue.)
Spread the bread croûtes with mustard mayonnaise and a little relish;
place a slice of pickle on top. Finally, add a slice of tomato and the hot
mini hamburgers. Garnish with strips of scallion.

MOSTLY VEGETABLE

Left to right: *Cheese Balls with Paprika; Tabouli Bites; Ratatouille Bouchées; Watercress Roulade with Tomato and Cream Cheese; Cherry Tomatoes with Avocado.*

WATERCRESS, CREAM CHEESE AND TOMATO ROULADE

1 bunch watercress, washed
1 tbsp minced parsley
1 tbsp grated Parmesan cheese
2 eggs, separated
8 oz cream cheese, softened with milk
2 tomatoes, skinned, deseeded and chopped
Salt and freshly ground black pepper

Preheat the oven to 375°F. Line a jelly roll pan, roughly 8×12 inches with greased parchment paper. Remove the stalks from the watercress and dry thoroughly. Chop and mix with the parsley, Parmesan cheese and egg yolks. Beat well and season. Whisk the egg whites until stiff and fold into the watercress mixture. Turn into the pan and bake for 10-12 minutes. Cool. Mix the cream cheese with the tomato and season with salt and pepper. Lay the cold roulade on a sheet of parchment paper. Peel off the lining paper and spread with the cream cheese mixture. Roll up like a tiny jelly roll. Trim the untidy edges and cut into about 20 smaller rolls.

GARLIC MUSHROOMS IN BREAD CRUMBS

20 even-sized mushrooms
2 cloves garlic, crushed
2 tsp minced parsley
1 stick (4 oz) butter, softened
Salt, freshly ground black pepper
1 tsp lemon juice
Flour
1 egg, beaten with a little milk
Dry white bread crumbs
Oil for deep-frying

Wipe the mushrooms and remove the stems. Add the garlic and parsley to the butter and season with salt, black pepper and lemon juice. Turn the mushrooms cap-side down and place a dab of butter in the cavity left by the stem. Mix the egg with a pinch of salt. Dip the mushrooms first into flour, then into the egg and milk, and finally into the bread crumbs. Chill for 1 hour. Heat the oil until a piece of bread dropped in will sizzle vigorously. Fry the mushrooms until golden-brown, drain on paper towels and sprinkle with salt. Serve immediately.

SPINACH AND RICOTTA FILO TRIANGLES

4 oz frozen chopped spinach
1 stick (4 oz) butter
¼ lb Ricotta cheese
Salt, black pepper and ground nutmeg
8 sheets filo pastry

Defrost the spinach. Melt 2 tbsp butter in a heavy pan, add the spinach and heat, stirring constantly, until any liquid has boiled away. Stir in the Ricotta cheese and season. Melt the remaining butter. Lay half the sheets of filo pastry on the work surface and brush with butter, cover with the remaining sheets of pastry and more melted butter. Cut each pair of pastry sheets lengthwise into five strips. Place a spoonful of filling at one end of each strip. Form a triangle by folding the right-hand corner to the opposite side, then fold over and then across from the left-hand corner to the right edge. Continue folding until the strip of pastry is used up. Preheat the oven to 400°F. Place the filo triangles on a greased baking sheet. Brush with melted butter and bake for about 10 minutes until golden-brown. Serve warm.

TIP: See p.67 for details on storing and freezing filo triangles.

CREAM PUFFS WITH STILTON SALAD

20 cream puffs (see recipe p.146)
¼ lb grated Stilton cheese
1 stalk celery, chopped
2 tsp snipped chives
6 walnuts, chopped
1 tsp walnut oil
Squeeze of lemon juice
Salt and freshly ground black pepper

Mix the grated Stilton, chopped celery, chives and walnuts together. Moisten with the oil and lemon juice and season with salt and pepper. Make a diagonal slit through each puff from the top down towards the bottom. Pile in the Stilton salad and serve immediately.

TIP: Cream puffs freeze very well tightly wrapped in a plastic bag. Pop them frozen into a moderate oven (375°F) for 10 minutes to defrost and crisp before serving.

SEASONED CHEESE BALLS

1 lb cream cheese
¼ cup grated Cheddar cheese
½ tsp Dijon mustard
Pinch of cayenne pepper
Salt and freshly ground black pepper
2 oz Roquefort cheese
1 tbsp mixed chopped parsley, chervil and
    chives
1 small clove garlic, crushed
FOR GARNISH
1 tbsp paprika
1 tbsp toasted sesame seeds
1 tbsp minced parsley

Divide the cream cheese into 4 separate batches and place each in a bowl. Mix the Cheddar cheese, Dijon mustard and cayenne pepper with one batch and season with salt and black pepper. Mix the Roquefort cheese into the second batch, the chopped herbs and garlic into the third, and leave the last batch plain. Roll all the different cheeses into about 40 balls, keeping them in separate batches. Lightly dust the Cheddar-flavored ones with paprika, the Roquefort with sesame seeds, the herb and garlic cheese with parsley, and the plain ones with black pepper. Serve them mixed together in a basket lined with a napkin or, better still, with vine leaves.

TIP: The cheese can be flavored and shaped the day before but not finished until the day of the party.

MUSHROOM AND ROQUEFORT STRUDELS

20 even-sized mushrooms
¼ lb Roquefort cheese, softened (or other soft blue cheese)
8 sheets filo pastry
1 stick (4 oz) butter, melted
Salt and freshly ground black pepper
Beaten egg

Preheat the oven to 400°F. Grease a baking sheet. Wipe the mushrooms and carefully remove the stems. Fill the caps with Roquefort cheese. Brush half the sheets of pastry with melted butter, then add a second sheet to each one. Brush again with butter. Cut the sheets of filo pastry into small squares. Put a filled mushroom in the center of each square and season with salt and pepper. Draw the edges of the pastry up together to look like a small sack. Pinch the "neck" together firmly with the fingers. Place on the baking sheet and brush with beaten egg. Bake for 15-20 minutes until the pastry is golden-brown. Serve immediately.

TIP: The strudels can be prepared, but not baked, the day before.

TABOULI BITES

⅓ cup cracked wheat
2 cucumbers
2 small tomatoes, skinned, deseeded and
    chopped
½ green pepper, deseeded and chopped
1 shallot, minced
1 tbsp chopped fresh mint
1 tbsp minced parlsey or cilantro
2 tbsp olive oil
Salt, freshly ground black pepper and
    lemon juice

Soak the cracked wheat in cold water for 1 hour. Drain well, wrap in a clean tea towel and squeeze out all the excess moisture. Spread the wheat on a tray to dry. Cut the cucumbers in half lengthwise and scoop out the seeds with a teaspoon. Put all the prepared vegetables into a mixing bowl with the soaked wheat; add the mint, parsley and oil. Season well with salt, black pepper and lemon juice. Spoon the tabouli into the hollowed-out cucumbers and cut each half into about 5 pieces.

TORTELLONI WITH HOT PROVENÇALE PEPPER DIP

5 tbsp olive oil
1 small onion, minced
2 cloves garlic, crushed
1 green pepper, deseeded and chopped
1 red pepper, deseeded and chopped
1 8-oz can tomatoes
½ tsp marjoram and 1 tsp basil
Salt and freshly ground black pepper
40 fresh tortelloni (any type will do)

Heat 3 tbsp oil in a heavy pan. Add the onion and garlic and fry gently until soft and transparent. Stir in the peppers, tomatoes, marjoram and basil and season with salt and pepper. Simmer gently until the dip is well-reduced, dark and oily. Bring a large pan of salted water to a boil and add 1 tbsp oil. Cook the tortelloni until tender (about 12 minutes). Drain and rinse with boiling water. Return to the pan and toss in a little oil. Thread onto cocktail toothpicks and serve with the hot Provençale pepper dip in a small dish.

CAMEMBERT PASTRY PARCELS

½ Camembert cheese, well-chilled
1 recipe quantity cheese pastry (p.147)
2 tbsp good quality gooseberry preserves
1 egg, beaten

Cut the Camembert cheese into 1-inch cubes. Roll the pastry out thinly and cut into 3-inch squares. Put a little gooseberry preserves in the center of each square and top with a cube of cheese. Brush the edges of the pastry with beaten egg and draw them up to the top to make a parcel resembling a small sack. Pinch the "neck" tightly together and snip off the excess pastry (it is vital to seal the parcel or the cheese will leak out). Preheat the oven to 400°F. Grease a baking sheet. Brush the Camembert parcels with beaten egg, place on the baking sheet and bake for 10-15 minutes, until the pastry is golden-brown. Serve the parcels immediately.

TIP: The pastry parcels can be made the day before and chilled overnight.

QUAIL-EGG FLOWERS

10 small fat pickling cucumbers
⅔ cup wine vinegar
⅔ cup water
¾ cup sugar
2 tbsp salt
2 tbsp oil
2 cloves garlic, crushed
1 tsp crushed black peppercorns
Good pinch ground coriander
⅔ cup soy sauce
2 tbsp brown sugar
20 quails' eggs, hard-cooked and peeled

Cut 1 inch from the ends of each cucumber (the middles can be used to make Tabouli Bites (p.79). With a melon-baller, scoop most of the flesh out of the cucumber ends to make little cups. With a sharp knife, cut deep zig-zags from the rim of the cucumber to look like petals. Mix the vinegar, water, sugar and half the salt together and soak the cucumber flowers in this for 30 minutes. Heat the oil in a skillet and add the remaining salt, garlic, peppercorns, coriander, soy sauce and brown sugar. Turn the quails' eggs in the hot soy sauce mixture until evenly

brown. Allow the eggs to cool in the sauce, turning them occasionally.
Drain the cucumber flowers well and put a quails' egg into each one.
Spear with a cocktail toothpick through the base of the cucumber into
the quails' egg, to resemble a stalk. Or, alternatively, slice a little off
the base of the cucumber flowers so that they will sit flat and arrange
them on a plate.

TIP: To hard-cook quails' eggs, boil them gently for 3 minutes.

CHÈVRE TARTS

1 recipe quantity cheese pastry, (see
    recipe p.147)
½ lb soft goat's cheese
1 red apple
6 walnuts, chopped
Walnut oil
Squeeze of lemon juice
Salt and freshly ground black pepper

Preheat the oven to 400°F. Roll the pastry thinly and stamp out 2-inch circles. Press into tiny patty pans and chill for 30 minutes. Fill each pastry shell with a crumpled piece of aluminum foil and bake for 10-15 minutes. Cool. Cut the goat's cheese into ¼-inch dice. Cut the apple, with the skin on, into pea-sized balls with a mini melon-baller. Place the goat's cheese, apple and walnuts together in a bowl and moisten with the oil and lemon juice. Season with salt and pepper. Spoon into the pastry shells and serve immediately.

TIP: If baking several batches of pastry shells at one time, stack the pans on top of each other instead of filling with foil. The filling will soon discolor, so this recipe is not very suitable for large parties.

BELGIAN ENDIVE WITH COTTAGE CHEESE, ORANGE AND WALNUTS

2 heads Belgian endive
2 small oranges
⅔ cup cottage cheese
6 walnuts, finely chopped
1 tsp minced parsley
Salt and freshly ground black pepper

Separate the endive leaves and wash and dry them. Use only the smaller leaves. Grate the rind from the oranges and add it to the cottage cheese together with the walnuts and chopped parsley. Season with salt and pepper. Peel the oranges with a sharp knife and cut into sections, discarding all the pith and seeds. Drain the sections on paper towels. Spoon a little of the cottage cheese mixture into each endive leaf and set an orange section on top.

MINI FRIED GRUYÈRE SANDWICHES

6 slices soft white bread
Butter for spreading
Dijon mustard
¼ lb Gruyère cheese, thinly sliced

Butter the bread and lay half the slices butter-side down on the work surface. Spread the unbuttered side with a little mustard and cover with the cheese. Top with the remaining bread so that you have a sandwich with the butter on the outside. Heat a heavy skillet or griddle and fry the sandwiches slowly until they are golden-brown and the cheese inside has melted. Trim the crusts and cut each sandwich into 8 triangles. Serve immediately.

TIP: If preparing these for more than 20 people, preheat the oven to 425°F, put the sandwiches on a baking sheet and bake for 10 minutes on the first side and 5 minutes on the second.

FALAFEL

1 15-oz can garbanzo beans
1 egg, lightly beaten
½ tsp ground turmeric
2 tbsp chopped cilantro leaves
¼ tsp ground cumin
¼ tsp cayenne pepper
1 clove garlic, crushed
1 tbsp tahini (sesame seed paste)
2 rounded tbsp cracked wheat, soaked and
    squeezed dry
Salt and freshly ground black pepper
½ cup all-purpose flour
Oil for deep-frying

Put the garbanzo beans into a food processor or blender with the egg, turmeric, cilantro, cumin, cayenne pepper, garlic, tahini and soaked cracked wheat. Season with salt and pepper. Blend until smooth. Shape the mixture into small slightly flattened balls and dust heavily with seasoned flour. Heat the oil until a piece of bread dropped in will sizzle vigorously. Fry the balls until lightly browned. Drain well on paper towels and serve hot.

TEX-MEX MUFFINS WITH CHILI DIP

6 tbsp butter, softened
1 3-oz package cream cheese
1 small egg, beaten
½ cup self-raising flour
½ cup cornmeal
Pinch of salt
½ small green pepper, chopped
½ small red pepper, chopped
FOR THE DIP
1 tbsp olive oil
½ medium onion, minced
1 clove garlic, crushed
Pinch of chili powder
1 8-oz can tomatoes

Grease about 20 tiny patty tins. Preheat the oven to 350°F. Beat the butter and cream cheese together until light and fluffy. Beat in the egg. Mix the flour, cornmeal and salt together and gradually add to the butter and cream cheese mixture, stirring until well mixed. Add the peppers. Spoon the mixture into the pans. Bake for 20 minutes or until golden-brown.

TO MAKE THE DIP. Heat the oil in a skillet and in it gently brown the onion and garlic. Add the chili powder and continue to cook for another minute. Stir in the tomatoes and simmer for 30 minutes. Purée the dip in a blender and serve hot in a small bowl surrounded by the warm muffins skewered with a cocktail toothpick.

TIP: The muffins can be frozen, then defrosted and reheated in a moderate oven for a few minutes before serving.

MINI PITAS WITH NIÇOISE FILLING

5 round mini pita breads
1 7-oz can tuna fish, packed in oil
½ cucumber, chopped
3 small tomatoes, skinned, deseeded and chopped
½ small onion, minced
½ green pepper, deseeded and minced
½ cup chopped green beans, cooked
1 hard-cooked egg, finely chopped
Salt and freshly ground black pepper

Drain a little but not all of the oil from the tuna and mash well with the cucumber, tomatoes, onion, green pepper, green beans and hard-cooked egg. Season with salt and pepper. Cut the pita bread into quarters. Spoon a little of the filling into the pocket of the triangles of pita bread.

TIP: The filling can be prepared the day before. Cover it tightly with plastic wrap and chill overnight. But do not fill the pitas as they quickly curl at the edges.

CHERRY TOMATOES WITH AVOCADO

10 cherry tomatoes
1 very ripe avocado
2 oz cream cheese
Salt and freshly ground black pepper
Worcestershire sauce
Tabasco sauce
Lemon juice

Cut the tomatoes in half, scoop out the flesh and seeds and discard. Leave the tomato shells to drain, turned upside-down on a sheet of paper towel. Purée the avocado flesh in a blender or food processor. Add the cream cheese and continue to process until very smooth. Season to taste with salt, pepper, Worcestershire sauce, Tabasco sauce and plenty of lemon juice (as this prevents the avocado from turning brown). Place the avocado mixture in a pastry bag fitted with a fluted tip and pipe whirls into the tomato halves.

TIP: To save time, the tomatoes can be prepared the day before.

WALNUT AND CHÈVRE SABLÉS

¾ cup all-purpose flour
Pinch of salt, dry mustard and cayenne pepper
6 tbsp butter
¾ cup finely grated Cheddar cheese
2 tbsp crumbled goat's cheese
¼ cup chopped walnuts

Sift the flour and seasonings into a mixing bowl. Dice the butter, then rub into the flour. When lumps of dough start to form, add the cheese and carefully draw the dough together, using the fingertips only. Knead gently and roll out on a lightly floured surface to approximately 1/8-inch thick. Stamp out 1-inch circles with a plain pastry cutter, place on a baking sheet and chill for 1 hour. Preheat the oven to 400°F. Mix the goat's cheese and walnuts together and sprinkle a little on top of each sablé. Bake for about 10 minutes, until golden-brown. Serve warm or cold.

TIP: This dough is very rich. Keep it cool and handle it as little as possible to prevent it from becoming greasy. The mixture can easily be made by combining all the ingredients in a food processor. The sablés can be stored overnight in an airtight container.

RATATOUILLE BOUCHÉES

1 small onion
1 clove garlic, crushed
½ small eggplant
½ zucchini
1 small green pepper, deseeded
1 8-oz can tomatoes
1 tbsp olive oil
Salt and freshly ground black pepper
Dried basil
20 baked patty shells (see recipe p.149)

Chop all the vegetables very finely. Heat the oil in a heavy pan, add the onion and garlic and fry gently until soft and transparent. Add the eggplant, zucchini and green pepper, cover the pan and continue to cook gently for 10 minutes. Add the tomatoes, season with salt, pepper and basil, bring to a boil and simmer until the vegetables are cooked and the ratatouille is well-reduced and shiny. If serving cold, allow the ratatouille to cool completely before using. To serve hot, warm the baked patty shells and fill with spoonfuls of hot ratatouille.
TIP: Ratatouille freezes well.

EGGPLANT SAMOSAS

2 cups all-purpose flour
½ tsp salt
¼ cup vegetable oil
¼ cup water
FOR THE FILLING
1 tbsp oil
1 medium-sized eggplant, pared and minced
1 clove garlic, crushed
¼ tsp ground allspice
¼ tsp marjoram
Salt and freshly ground black pepper
1 tsp tomato paste
Oil for deep-frying

Sift the flour and salt into a bowl and add the oil. Rub it in until the mixture resembles coarse bread crumbs. Slowly add the water while mixing the dough to a stiff ball with the fingertips. Knead for about 10 minutes. Rub a little extra oil over the dough, wrap it in plastic and leave to rest for at least 30 minutes. Meanwhile, make the filling: Heat the oil, add the eggplant, garlic, allspice and marjoram and season with salt and pepper. Sauté the mixture gently until soft and well-cooked. Stir in the tomato paste. Leave to cool.

Knead the dough again and divide into 10 balls. Roll them out thinly to about 4 inches in diameter and cut in half. Spoon a little filling on to one side of each piece of pastry, dampen the edges and fold over to form triangles. Press the edges well together, marking a pattern with a knife or fork. Heat the oil until a cube of bread dropped in will sizzle vigorously. Fry the samosas until golden-brown. Drain on paper towels and serve immediately, or leave to cool and serve at room temperature.

TIP: Samosas can also be made with the spinach and Ricotta filling (p.74) or the lamb filling (p.66).

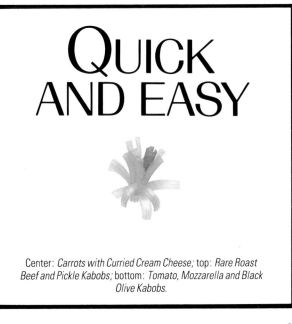

QUICK
AND EASY

Center: *Carrots with Curried Cream Cheese;* top: *Rare Roast Beef and Pickle Kabobs;* bottom: *Tomato, Mozzarella and Black Olive Kabobs.*

PROSCIUTTO-FRUIT BUNDLES

Wedge of ripe melon
½ ripe papaya
2 fresh figs
6 oz prosciutto, very thinly sliced

Remove the skin and seeds from the melon and papaya and scoop into balls with a melon baller. Cut the figs into bite-sized chunks. Slice the prosciutto into strips about 1 inch wide. Wrap each piece of fruit neatly in a strip of prosciutto and secure with a cocktail toothpick.

STUFFED SNOW PEAS

20 small fresh snow peas
¼ lb Boursin cheese
Milk

Top and tail the snow peas and plunge them into boiling salted water for 3 minutes, then immediately into cold water. Drain and pat dry with paper towels. With a very sharp vegetable parer, split the snow peas on the curved side. Soften the cheese with a little milk and place in a large pastry bag fitted with a medium plain tip. Pipe a squiggle of cheese into each snow pea.

TIP: To save time, the snow peas can be prepared the day before.

SARDINE CRESCENTS

4 oz puff pastry
3 oz canned sardines
Salt, freshly ground black pepper and
lemon juice
1 egg, beaten

Roll the pastry out thinly. Drain and mash the sardines and season with salt, pepper and lemon juice. Spread the mixture over the pastry and fold in half. Roll into a rectangle, fold into three, turn so that the folded edge is to the left and roll again. Cut out crescent shapes by stamping a semicircle with a 2-inch plain pastry cutter at one edge of the pastry. Then place the cutter partially over the cut round edge of the pastry strip so that the next cut will make a crescent shape. Continue to cut until all the pastry is used. Place on a damp baking sheet and chill for 30 minutes. Preheat the oven to 400°F. Brush with beaten egg and bake for 15-20 minutes until golden-brown. Serve hot.
TIP: The sardine crescents can be baked the day before and reheated on the day of the party.

FRESH DATES STUFFED WITH CREAM CHEESE AND ALMONDS

20 fresh dates
8 oz cream cheese
Milk
¼ cup ground almonds
1 cup toasted, chopped almonds

With a sharp vegetable parer, split the dates lengthwise along the top and remove the pit. Soften the cream cheese with a little milk and stir in the ground almonds. Place this mixture in a pastry bag fitted with a fluted tip and pipe lines of it into the dates. After each date is filled, dip the top of the cream cheese into the toasted almonds so that it becomes coated in nuts.

SHRIMP AND SCALLOPS IN GARLIC BUTTER

(About 40 mouthfuls)
20 bay scallops
3 scallions, cleaned and trimmed
2 tbsp olive oil
2 tbsp butter
3 cloves garlic, crushed
3 tbsp dry vermouth
¾ lb shelled, boiled shrimp

Remove the tough muscle opposite the coral from the scallops. Cut the scallions into thin strips. Heat the oil and butter in a heavy-based skillet and gently sauté the garlic. Pour in the vermouth and simmer until the liquid is reduced to about 2 tablespoonful and buttery. Add the scallops and toss over the heat for a few minutes until cooked. Stir in the shrimp and scallions and cook for an additional few minutes, until heated through. Serve the shrimp and scallops in the pan in which they were cooked, handing cocktail toothpicks for the guests to help themselves.

TUNA TOASTS

1 package melba toasts (bought from a delicatessen)
1 7-oz can tuna fish
½ small onion, minced
2 tbsp mayonnaise
Salt and freshly ground black pepper
Cayenne pepper

With a sharp knife, cut the melba toast into small rectangles. Drain the tuna fish well and mash with the onion. Stir in the mayonnaise and season with salt and pepper. Place a spoonful on top of each melba toast and garnish with a tiny sprinkle of cayenne pepper.

CARROTS WITH CURRIED CREAM CHEESE

3 medium-sized carrots
8 oz cream cheese
Milk
Curry powder
Salt and freshly ground black pepper
Cilantro leaves

Pare the carrots. With the tip of a vegetable or citrus peeler, cut grooves down the length of the carrot and all the way around. Slice the carrots about ¼-inch thick. Soften the cream cheese with milk and flavor with curry paste. Place in a pastry bag fitted with a fluted tip and pipe whirls on to the carrot slices. Garnish with whole cilantro leaves.

Mini Pizzas

20 dried bread croûtes (see recipe p.150)
3 oz strong Cheddar cheese, finely
*   sliced*
1 tsp oregano
4 small tomatoes, skinned and sliced
10 pitted black olives, halved

Put a slice of tomato on each of the dried bread croûtes. Cut the cheese into small squares and lay on top of the tomato. Sprinkle with oregano and garnish with half a black olive. Broil the mini pizzas under a hot broiler until the cheese has melted. Serve immediately.

TIP: The mini pizzas can be broiled before the party and left to cool. Reheat them in a moderate oven just before serving.

TOMATO, MOZZARELLA AND BLACK OLIVE KABOBS

4 oz Mozzarella cheese
2 tomatoes, peeled
10 black olives, pitted and halved

Cut the Mozzarella into ½-inch cubes. Cut the tomatoes in half. Remove the seeds and cut the flesh of each tomato into 10 strips. Thread a cube of Mozzarella on to each cocktail toothpick, followed by a strip of tomato and finally a black olive.

TIP: Try to buy Mozzarella cheese that is fairly firm or it may break when threaded on to the cocktail toothpicks.

MELON AND HONEY-BAKED HAM KABOBS

½ honeydew melon
½ lb honey-baked ham, in one piece

Scrape the seeds from the melon and scoop the flesh into balls with a melon-baller. Cut the ham into ½-inch cubes. Thread the melon balls and ham cubes alternately on to cocktail toothpicks.

TIP: Don't push the cocktail toothpick right through the food as it will be awkward to eat. The traditional way of serving cocktail kabobs is porcupine-style with the toothpicks stuck into an upturned melon, cabbage or pineapple. Or serve them with other items arranged in rows on serving dish.

ASSORTED MINI SANDWICHES

(Each filling is enough for 5 sandwiches or 20 mini sandwiches)

CELERIAC FILLING
½ lb Celeriac (celery root), thickly pared and grated
2 tbsp thick mayonnaise
½ tsp Dijon mustard
1 tsp capers, finely chopped
1 tsp chopped gherkins
Salt and freshly ground black pepper

CREAM CHEESE, TOMATO AND CHIVE FILLING
3 oz cream cheese
Milk
2 tomatoes, skinned, deseeded and chopped
1 heaping tbsp snipped chives
Salt and freshly ground black pepper

SARDINE AND EGG FILLING
5 oz canned sardines in oil, drained and mashed
2 hard-cooked eggs, chopped
Salt and freshly ground black pepper

SALMON AND WATERCRESS FILLING

8-oz can salmon or fresh salmon, cooked and flaked
½ bunch watercress, stalks removed, washed and
chopped
Salt, freshly ground black pepper and lemon juice
TO GARNISH
Watercress, radish slices, alfalfa sprouts, whole
olives

Two slices of bread, filled, will cut into four mini sandwiches. Any thinly sliced bread is suitable, all sorts of cracked wheat, wholewheat, pumpernickel and other types are now available sliced. Choose a color to compliment the filling. For instance, the celeriac filling will look pale brownish and therefore will look more attractive between white bread than brown. Spread the bread with softened butter. Don't skimp on the butter – after all it is an ingredient of any sandwich and will also prevent moisture from the fillings soaking into the bread.

The fillings are made by mixing all the ingredients together and seasoning to taste. Use them generously. When the sandwiches are made, trim the crusts so that you have a completely square sandwich. Cut each one into four triangles. Set them upright on a platter so the filling can be seen. The effect of this is best with alternate rows of brown and white sandwiches. Garnish with watercress, alfalfa sprouts, radish slices or whole olives.

TIP: An electric carving knife makes it much easier to cut perfectly neat sandwiches. Once made, cover the sandwiches with a damp towel to keep them fresh.

Other recipes that could be used as sandwich fillings are Smoked Trout Mousse (p.20), Ham, Cream Cheese and Chives (p.65), Smoked Chicken (p.62), Chicken and Lobster (p.68), Pâté (p.48), Avocado (p.91), Niçoise (p.90), Cottage Cheese, Orange and Walnuts (p.85), and Tuna Fish (p.103).

FRENCH BREAD OPEN FACE SANDWICHES

A party can be quickly put together by serving French bread with almost anything that can be bought from the local grocery. The trick is to buy a very fresh, narrow French bread, about 2 inches in diameter and slice it about ¼-inch thick. For a casual party, the bread can be buttered and spread with pâté and garnished with an olive, topped with a thin slice of Brie cheese and a twist of cucumber, or herring in sour cream with rings of raw onion. For a more sophisticated effect, the top should be completely covered. Use thin slices of smoked salmon, smoked halibut, prosciutto, German salami or raw beef (p.60) stamped out with a sharp pastry cutter to fit the slice of French bread exactly. Garnish the fish filling with a sprig of dill or a spoonful of real or mock caviar. Meat fillings can be garnished with mustard or herb mayonnaise.

ASPARAGUS AND PROSCIUTTO

20 spears fresh asparagus, cooked
6 oz prosciutto, thinly sliced
Freshly ground black pepper

Trim the tough stalks from the asparagus so that the spears measure about 3 inches. Sprinkle with black pepper. Cut the prosciutto into strips about 2 inches wide. Wrap the strips around the asparagus spears so that a little asparagus is showing at each end.

BEETS WITH HORSERADISH CREAM CHEESE

10 slices light rye bread
6 oz cream cheese
Milk
Horseradish relish
½ lb cooked whole beets, peeled

Stamp two 2-inch circles out of each slice of bread. Soften the cream cheese with the milk and flavor with horseradish. Spread this mixture over the rounds of bread. Slice the beets and cut into neat squares. Use to garnish the canapés just before serving.

TIP: It is sometimes possible to buy cream cheese that is already flavored with horseradish.

SPICED NIBBLES

½ lb dried garbanzo beans
1 slice bacon, chopped
6 tbsp peanut oil
Good pinch of chili powder
1 tsp paprika
1 tsp tomato paste
Salt and freshly ground black pepper
½ lb whole blanched almonds
6 tbsp sugar
1 tsp ground cumin
Oil for deep-frying
½ lb cashew nuts

Soak the garbanzo beans overnight. Drain and cook in boiling water with the bacon until they are tender. Drain well and pat dry with paper towels. Heat 3 tbsp of the peanut oil in a skillet and add a pinch of chili powder, the paprika and tomato paste. Gently fry the garbanzos in the spice mixture until they are well-covered and soaked in oil. Drain, sprinkle with salt and pepper and leave to cool. Heat the remaining peanut oil, add the almonds and sprinkle the sugar over. Fry gently until the almonds become golden-brown and the sugar caramelizes. Put the almonds in a bowl and toss with the cumin and 1 tsp of salt. Serve warm or cold.

Heat the oil for deep-frying until a cube of bread dropped in will sizzle vigorously. Add the cashew nuts and fry until deep golden-brown. Remove from the oil immediately, drain well and spread on paper towels. Sprinkle with plenty of salt, pepper and a pinch of chili powder. They can be served warm or cold.

TIP: The almonds and cashew nuts can be stored for up to two weeks in airtight containers.

BACON AND SCALLOP ROLLS

10 slices bacon
20 bay scallops
Salt
Freshly ground black pepper
Lemon juice

Stretch each slice of bacon with the back of a knife and cut in half. Remove the tough muscle opposite the coral. Season the scallops with salt, pepper and lemon juice. Wrap a piece of bacon tightly around each scallop and pack loosely together in a roasting pan with the seam underneath to stop them from unravelling. Heat the broiler to the highest temperature and broil the bacon rolls for 5-10 minutes, turning halfway through the cooking, until crisp and brown. Serve immediately, skewered with a cocktail toothpick, or leave in a cool place and reheat for 5 minutes in a hot oven just before serving.

TIP: Bacon rolls can be prepared the day before but should be cooked on the day of the party.

BACON AND BANANA ROLLS

10 slices bacon
2 bananas
Salt and freshly ground black pepper

Stretch each slice of bacon with the back of a knife and cut in half. Cut the bananas into chunks. Wrap a piece of bacon tightly around each and pack loosely together in a roasting pan, with the seam underneath to stop them from unravelling. Heat the broiler to the highest temperature and broil the bacon rolls for 5-10 minutes, turning halfway through cooking, until crisp and brown. Serve immediately, skewered with a cocktail toothpick, or leave in a cool place and reheat for 5 minutes in a hot oven just before serving.

TIP: These rolls can also be made with chunks of lychee fruit instead of the banana.

Puff Pastry Anchovies

4 oz puff pastry
Anchovy paste
Superfine sugar
1 egg, beaten

Roll the pastry out thinly and spread with a thin layer of anchovy paste. Sprinkle with sugar. Fold in half and roll into a rectangle. Fold the strip into three, turn so that the folded edge is to the left and roll again. Stamp out fish shapes with a shaped pastry cutter and place on a damp baking sheet. Chill for 30 minutes. Preheat the oven to 400°F. Brush with beaten egg and bake for 15 minutes until golden-brown. Serve hot.

TIP: Any shape cutter can be used to make the anchovies or the pastry can be cut into fingers. The pastries can be made the day before, stored in an airtight container overnight, and reheated before serving.

QUAILS' AND GULLS' EGGS WITH CHILI DIP

20 quails' eggs
20 gulls' eggs
Celery salt, sea salt
    or chili dip (see recipe p.88)

Gently boil the quails' eggs for 3 minutes. Drain them, cover with cold water and leave to cool. Gulls' eggs are bought ready-cooked. Serve them in their shells (with a separate dish for the debris) with the celery salt, sea salt or chili dip in a small dish on the side.

JUMBO SHRIMP WITH AÏOLI DIP

20 fresh jumbo shrimp, boiled
FOR THE AÏOLI DIP
3 cloves garlic, crushed
2 egg yolks
Pinch of salt
1 tsp Dijon mustard
⅔ cup each olive oil and salad oil
Squeeze of lemon juice
2 tbsp wine vinegar
Freshly ground black pepper

Carefully peel the shrimp, leaving the heads intact. Place the garlic, egg yolks, salt and mustard in a mixing bowl or in the bowl of a food processor. Gradually add the oil, drop by drop, beating constantly. The mixture should become very thick by the time half the oil is added. Stir in the lemon juice and vinegar. Add the remaining oil in a steady stream. Season with salt and pepper. Spoon the aïoli into a small dish and place in the center of a round flat serving dish. Arrange the peeled shrimp around the edge of the dip.

RARE ROAST BEEF AND PICKLE KABOBS

½ lb sliced rare roast beef
4 dill pickles

With a very sharp knife, cut the beef into 1-inch strips. Cut the dill pickles into 20 chunks. Pleat the strips of meat on to cocktail toothpicks and thread a chunk of pickle on to each one.

TIP: Pastrami makes a delicious substitute for the roast beef.

CRUDITÉS

A selection of raw vegetables
½ cucumber, cut into sticks
2 carrots, pared and cut into sticks
½ green pepper, deseeded and cut into sticks
½ red pepper, deseeded and cut into sticks
1 bunch scallions, cleaned and trimmed
12 cherry tomatoes
¼ lb button mushrooms
1 bunch radishes, with a little stalk left on
¼ cauliflower, cut into florets

Prepare the vegetables and arrange them in clusters on a round plate, leaving room for a bowl of dip in the center. If preparing them in advance, form the vegetable sticks into bundles and secure at each end with a rubber band. Keep in a bowl of ice water.

The vegetables listed above are the most commonly used for crudités, but more unusual ones can be offered too, such as sticks of eggplant, turnip, baby beets, green beans, snow peas. One attractive idea is to choose vegetables on a particular color scheme: green, purple (eggplant, red cabbage, beets, purple beans) or red and white, etc.

HOT BRIE OR CAMEMBERT DIP

1 whole Camembert or baby Brie cheese

Lift the cheese out of its box, remove the wrapping and rewrap in aluminum foil. Replace in the box without the lid. Preheat the oven to 375°F and bake the cheese for about 20 minutes, until it is warm and runny. With a sharp knife, remove the crust from the top of the cheese and set in the center of the crudités. If the cheese starts to cool and harden, warm it again in the oven.

SPINACH AND BOURSIN DIP

4 oz frozen chopped spinach
2 oz Boursin cheese and 2 oz cream cheese
Milk
Salt, freshly ground black pepper, nutmeg

Defrost the spinach, squeeze very dry and drain on paper towels. Mix together the Boursin and cream cheese and soften with a little milk. Beat in the spinach and season with salt, pepper and nutmeg.

CARROT AND CARDAMOM DIP

½ lb carrots
1 tbsp butter
1¼ cups water
1 bay leaf and 2 cardamom pods
2 tbsp Greek yogurt
2 tsp minced chervil
Salt and freshly ground black pepper

Pare and slice the carrots. Melt the butter in a pan, add the carrots, cover and cook gently for 10 minutes. Add the water, bay leaf and cardamom pods and simmer until the carrots are tender. Strain, remove the bay leaf and cardamom and leave to cool. Purée with the yogurt, stir in the chervil and season to taste with salt and pepper.

SMOKED SAUSAGE, BACON AND PEPPER KABOBS

8 oz spicy smoked sausage
4 slices bacon
½ red pepper
½ green pepper

Cut the smoked sausage into 20 chunks. Broil the bacon until golden-brown and cut it into ½-inch pieces. Deseed the peppers and cut into pieces about the same size as the bacon. Arrange on cocktail tooth-picks. Preheat the oven to 375°F and just before serving, bake the smoked sausage kabobs for 10 minutes.

TIP: Almost any type of smoked sausage is suitable for this recipe. Kabanos, Polish pork sausages, are highly spiced and particularly good.

ASPARAGUS CROUSTADE

5 slices brown bread, crusts removed
Butter for spreading
10 spears canned asparagus
Freshly ground black pepper

Flatten the bread with a rolling pin. Butter each slice, cut in half and lay the slices, butter-side down, on the work surface. Drain the asparagus well and pat dry with paper towels. Place an asparagus spear along the edge of each slice of bread, season with pepper and roll up tightly. Cut each roll in half and set on a baking sheet. Chill for 30 minutes. Preheat the oven to 425°F and bake the croustades until crisp and golden-brown. Serve hot or cold.

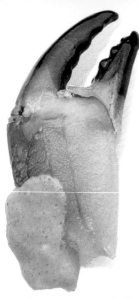

CRAB CLAWS DIPPED IN SMOKED COD ROE SAUCE

20 crab claws, shells removed but with the tips of the claws intact
Lemon juice
Freshly ground black pepper
FOR THE SAUCE
2 oz smoked cod roe, skinned
Freshly ground black pepper
1 shallot, minced
1 clove garlic, crushed
Juice of ½ lemon
1 tsp tomato paste
Dash of Worcestershire sauce
Dash of Tabasco sauce
⅔ cup heavy cream, lightly whipped
1 tsp mayonnaise

If using frozen crab claws, defrost them slowly overnight, sprinkled with lemon juice and pepper. Place the cod roe, shallot, garlic, lemon juice and tomato paste into a blender or food processor and blend until smooth. Pour the mixture into a bowl and season with Worcestershire sauce, Tabasco sauce and pepper. Fold in the whipped cream and mayonnaise. Serve the sauce in a small bowl set in the center of a serving dish surrounded by the crab claws.

TIP: Crab claws usually are sold frozen and ready-prepared for cocktail parties with the tip of the claw attached to the shelled white meat. It is a good idea to order them in advance. Don't forget to have a dish handy for guests to put the shells in.

MEXICAN TOSTADAS

20 dried bread croûtes (see recipe p.150)
2 cocktail avocados
1 cup finely grated Cheddar cheese
20 slices of garlic sausage, approx 1½
*   inches in diameter*
1 tbsp mayonnaise

Peel the cocktail avocados and cut each one into 10 slices. Heat the broiler. Spread a little mayonnaise on each of the dried bread croûtes, then cover with a slice of garlic sausage, followed by a slice of avocado. Sprinkle with grated cheese and place under the broiler until the cheese has melted. Serve immediately.

BRIE AND BLACK GRAPES

¼ medium-ripe Brie cheese
20 black grapes, halved and deseeded

Cut the Brie cheese into 20 cubes, each about ½ inch. Thread half a black grape on to a cocktail toothpick, followed by a cube of Brie and then another half black grape. Arrange the grapes so that the cut ends face the cheese.

TIP: The grapes can be prepared in advance but the Brie must be cut on the day of the party.

Sweet

From the outside: *Caramel Cream Puffs; Strawberry Tartlets; Walnut and Lemon Curd Mini Meringues.*

FRUIT FONDUE

A selection of fruit: Cantaloupe, apples, bananas,
   oranges, black grapes, strawberries, cherries
Lemon juice
FOR THE DIPS
4 oz semisweet chocolate
1 tbsp golden syrup or pancake syrup
2 tsp brandy
2 tbsp milk
2 cups heavy cream, whipped
⅔ cup cottage cheese, sieved
Confectioner's sugar to taste
Grated rind of 2 small oranges
6 tbsp orange juice

Chill the fruit for a few hours. Prepare it for eating with the fingers: peel and deseed the melon and cut the flesh into slices. Quarter, core and thickly slice the apples. Peel the bananas and cut into chunks. Break the oranges into sections, picking off any pith. Wash the grapes, strawberries and cherries, leaving the stalks on. Brush the apple and banana with lemon juice and arrange the fruits on a well-chilled dish. The dips are handed around separately to dunk the fruit in.

TO PREPARE THE DIPS: Place the chocolate, syrup, brandy and milk together in a small pan and melt over low heat, stirring occasionally until completely smooth. Serve warm. Fold one-third of the whipped cream into the sieved cottage cheese and sweeten to taste. Serve in a small bowl. Mix the remaining whipped cream with the orange rind and juice and sweeten with confectioner's sugar.

MINI MERINGUES

Makes about 10 of each type
3 egg whites
⅔ cup superfine sugar
2½ tbsp soft brown sugar
¼ cup finely ground walnuts
⅓ cup berries (strawberries, raspberries, etc.)
1 tbsp lemon curd
⅔ cup heavy cream, whipped
2 tbsp unsalted butter
½ cup confectioner's sugar, sifted
1 tsp coffee extract
½ egg yolk

Preheat the oven to 200°F. Cover a baking sheet with a sheet of oiled parchment paper. Beat the egg whites until stiff. Add 6 tbsp of the superfine sugar and continue to beat until very stiff and shiny. Divide the mixture into three. Add 2 tbsp sugar to one-third of the mixture; the brown sugar to the next third; and the remaining superfine sugar and ground walnuts to the last batch. Place the walnut meringues in small spoonfuls on the prepared baking sheet and pipe the other sorts with a fluted tip in little whirls. Bake them for about 1 hour. They are ready when light and dry and when the paper can be pulled off easily. Wash and coarsely chop the berries and mix with half the whipped cream. Use this mixture to sandwich the plain meringues together. Mix the lemon curd with the remaining cream and use as a filling for the walnut meringues. Soften the butter and beat in the remaining ingredients until light and fluffy. Sandwich the brown sugar meringues together with the coffee filling.

TIP: The plain and brown sugar meringues can be made in advance and stored for several weeks in an airtight container.

SWEET PANCAKES

*20 thin pancakes about 4 inches in
    diameter
2 oz Petit Suisse or cream cheese
Superfine sugar
2 tbsp whipped cream
1½ cups berries (strawberries,
    blueberries, etc.)
Jam the same flavor as the berries*

As soon as the pancakes are cooked, place them on a heated plate, cover and keep warm in a slow oven. Sweeten the Petit Suisse with superfine sugar and mix with the cream. To serve: put a dollop of the Petit Suisse mixture on one side of each pancake and top it with a smaller dollop of jam. Arrange a few berries on top of this and fold neatly.

TIP: Pancakes freeze well.

Golden Grapes

20 green grapes
1 cup granulated sugar
A little water

Place the sugar with a little water in a heavy-based pan, set over a very low heat and melt to a golden caramel. Dip the base of the pan in cold water to stop the cooking, then stand it in hot water to keep the caramel liquid. Dip the fruit into the caramel (taking great care not to touch the caramel with the fingertips) and leave to set on an oiled baking sheet.

TIP: Caramel is scorching hot and can cause serious burns so take great care when using it.

CARAMEL CREAM PUFFS

1 recipe quantity savory cream puff pastry
  (see recipe p.146), omitting the
  seasonings and Parmesan cheese
1¼ cups heavy cream, whipped
1 tbsp Grand Marnier liqueur
Grated rind of 2 oranges
½ cup granulated sugar

Preheat the oven to 400°F. Dampen two baking sheets. Put the cream puff pastry in a pastry bag with a fluted tip and pipe in rounds on to the baking sheets. Bake for 20-30 minutes, until puffed up and golden-brown. Remove from the oven and make a small slit in the side of each puff. Return to the oven to dry the insides. Cool on a wire rack.

Mix the whipped cream with the Grand Marnier and orange rind. Place in a pastry bag fitted with a medium-sized plain tip and fill the cream puffs through the small hole in the side. Set the wire rack with the cream puffs over an oiled baking sheet. Put the granulated sugar in a heavy-based pan, set over low heat and melt to a golden caramel. Dribble the caramel over the tops of the cream puffs.

TIP: See warning for using caramel, p.139.

EASY CHOCOLATE TRUFFLES

4 oz cream cheese
2¼ cups confectioner's sugar, sifted
8 oz semisweet chocolate
Vanilla extract
Cocoa powder, sifted, or chocolate sprinkles

Soften the cream cheese and gradually mix in the confectioner's sugar. Break the chocolate into small pieces and melt in a bowl set over a pan of simmering water. Stir the melted chocolate into the cream cheese mixture and add the vanilla extract. Roll into small balls and coat the truffles in cocoa or chocolate sprinkles. Chill for 2 hours before serving.

ALMOND TARTLETS

4 tbsp unsalted butter
¼ cup sugar
1 egg
Squeeze of lemon juice
½ cup ground almonds
20 unbaked pastry shells (see recipe p.151)
4 tbsp all-purpose flour, sifted
¼ cup slivered almonds
2 tbsp apricot jam, sieved

Preheat the oven to 375°F. Cream the butter and sugar together until light and fluffy. Gradually beat in the egg. Add the lemon juice and fold in the flour and ground almonds. Pipe or spoon into the pastry shells, filling each one to just below the top. Scatter with the slivered almonds and bake for 10-15 minutes until golden-brown. Remove from the oven and brush the tops with hot apricot jam.

STRAWBERRY TARTLETS

20 pastry shells (see recipe p. 151)
4 oz Petit Suisse or cream cheese
Superfine sugar to taste
Vanilla extract
20 medium-sized strawberries
Red currant jelly
Squeeze of lemon juice

Sweeten the Petit Suisse with sugar, add the vanilla and spread a little in the bottom of each pastry shell. Wash the strawberries if necessary and remove the hulls. Set a whole berry on top of each tartlet. Warm the redcurrant jelly with the squeeze of lemon juice and brush over the tartlets.

TIP: If making these in quantity, it is quicker to pipe the Petit Suisse mixture into the pastry shells, using a large plain tip.

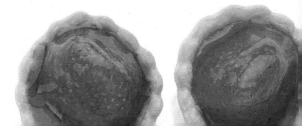

CURD MERINGUE TARTLETS

20 pastry shells (see recipe p.151)
2 small tangerines
¾ cup sugar
2 tbsp butter
1 tbsp lemon juice
2 eggs, separated

Wash and quarter the tangerines and "finely grind" them in a blender or food processor. Place in a bowl with 4 tbsp of sugar, the butter, lemon juice and egg yolks. Set the bowl over a pan of simmering water and stir gently until the mixture thickens slightly. Cool and spoon into the tartlet shells. Preheat the oven to 350°F. Beat the egg whites until stiff and gently fold in the remaining sugar. Place in a pastry bag fitted with a fluted tip and pipe in whirls on top of the tartlets. Bake in the oven for 15-20 minutes, until the meringue is brown on top.

BASES

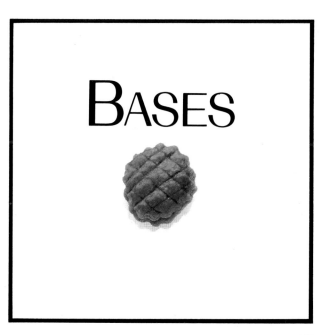

SAVORY CREAM PUFF PASTRY

⅔ cup all-purpose flour, sifted
Salt and freshly ground black pepper
Good pinch of dry mustard
Cayenne pepper
1 tsp Parmesan cheese
4 tbsp butter
⅔ cup water
2 eggs, beaten

Sift the flour with the seasonings and add the Parmesan cheese. Place the butter and water together in pan and bring slowly to a boil. As soon as the liquid boils, tip in all the flour at the same time, remove from the heat and beat the mixture until it becomes thick and leaves the sides of the pan. Leave to cool. Beat in the eggs a little at a time until the mixture is smooth and glossy. It may not be necessary to add all the eggs, the mixture should drop easily from a lifted spoon.

TO MAKE INTO CREAM PUFFS: Preheat the oven to 400°F. Pipe the pastry into small blobs on to a damp baking sheet. Brush with beaten egg and sprinkle with Parmesan cheese. Bake for 20-30 minutes, until puffed up and golden-brown. Remove from the oven and make a hole in the side of each puff. Return to the oven to dry the inside.

CHEESE PASTRY

1 cup all-purpose flour
4 tbsp butter
2 tbsp grated Parmesan cheese
Pinch of cayenne pepper
Pinch of dry mustard
½ egg, beaten
Cold water

Place the flour in a mixing bowl and rub in the butter. Add the Parmesan cheese, cayenne and mustard. Bind to a firm dough with the beaten egg and a little water. Knead gently.

TIP: The pastry can be frozen or made the day before.

TOASTIE CASES

10 slices bread
Butter for spreading

Preheat the oven to 425°F. Cut the bread into 2-inch circles with a plain pastry cutter. Spread the rounds with butter. Press them firmly into tiny patty pans, molding the bread to the shape of the pan and making the edges very thin. Bake in the hot oven until golden-brown and crisp. Remove from the pans and cool on a wire rack.

PATTY SHELLS

20 frozen patty shells
1 egg, beaten

Preheat the oven to 425°F. Place the patty shells on damp baking sheets and carefully brush the rims with beaten egg. Bake for 10-15 minutes, until well-risen and golden-brown. Remove from the oven and use the handle of a wooden spoon to push down the pastry in the center of each patty shell. Cool on a wire rack.

TIP: Patty shells can be made from puff pastry but ready-made frozen ones are both neat and quick to make. They can be bought in a variety of sizes – the smaller the better for cocktail recipes.

PUFF PASTRY CROÛTES

8 oz puff pastry

Roll the pastry out very thinly and stamp out circles with a 2-inch plain pastry cutter. Place them on a damp baking sheet and prick them all over. Chill for 1-2 hours. Preheat the oven to 425°F. Bake for 15 minutes until well-browned and crisp. Prick any that are very puffed up. Cool on a wire rack.

DRIED BREAD CROÛTES

Preheat the oven to 325°F. Cut any type of sliced bread into 1-inch circles. Place them on a baking sheet and bake until crisp and dry.

SWEET PASTRY SHELLS

1 cup all-purpose flour
4 tbsp butter
Pinch of superfine sugar
1 egg yolk
1 tbsp ice water

Sift the flour into a mixing bowl and rub in the butter. Add the egg yolk and enough water to bind to a firm dough. Roll out thinly and stamp out 2-inch circles with a fluted pastry cutter. Press into tiny patty pans and chill for 30 minutes. Preheat the oven to 400°F. Fill each pastry case with a crumpled piece of aluminum foil and bake for 10-15 minutes. Remove the foil halfway through baking to allow the pastry shells to dry out and become crisp and golden-brown.

Menu Suggestions

COCKTAIL PARTY
Smoked Trout Mousse and
   Smoked Salmon Parcels
New Potatoes with Sour Cream
   and Mock Caviar
Cherry Tomatoes with Avocado
Prosciutto-Fruit Bundles
Mini Antipasto
Cream Puffs with Stilton Salad
Red Lettuce with Salade Tiède
Herb-coated Knots of Flounder
   with Saffron Dip
Pork and Shrimp Toasts
Mushroom and Roquefort
   Strudels

BARBECUE PARTY
Pork and Mango with Saté Sauce
Mini Hamburgers
Kofta Kabobs
Tandoori Chicken with Cucumber
   and Yogurt Dip
Mini Barbecue Riblets
Nuggets of Marinated Lamb
Crudités
Spiced Nibbles
Mini Pitas with Niçoise Filling
Tex-Mex Muffins with Chili Dip
Curd Meringue Tartlets
Fruit Fondue

ITALIAN DRINKS PARTY
Asparagus and Prosciutto
Fritto Misto with Green
  Mayonnaise
Mini Antipasto
Mini Pizzas
Tuna Toasts
Tomato, Mozzarella and Black
  Olive Kabobs
Tortelloni with Hot Provençale
  Dip
Scallop Mousselinis
Garlic Mushrooms in
  Breadcrumbs

WEDDING RECEPTION
Smoked Salmon Wheels
Toasties with Pâté and Green
  Peppercorns
Carrots with Curried Cream
  Cheese
Mushroom and Oyster Bouchées
Bacon Rolls
Jumbo Shrimp with Aïoli Dip
Assorted Mini Sandwiches
French Bread Open Face
  Sandwiches
Strawberry Tartlets
Caramel Choux Puffs
Mini Meringues

FURTHER READING

Brennan, Jennifer, *Thai Cooking* (1981)
Haroutunian, Arto der, *Vegetarian Dishes from the Middle East* (1982)
Jaffrey, Madhur, *Indian Cookery* (1982)
Leith, Prue and Polly Tyrer, *Entertaining with Style* (1986)
Leith, Prue and Caroline Waldegrave, *Leith's Cookery Course* (1979)
Stewart, Martha, *Hors d'Oeuvres* (1985)
Worrall-Thompson, Antony, *The Small and Beautiful Cookbook* (1984)

RECIPE INDEX

Mini pitas with Niçoise filling, 90
Mini pizzas, 105
Moroccan lamb pies, 66-7
Mushroom and oyster bouchées, 42-3
Mushroom and Roquefort strudels, 78
Mussels in their shells with garlic butter, 25

New potatoes with sour cream and mock caviar, 36
Nuggets of marinated lamb, 64

Patty shells, 149
Pork and mango with saté sauce, 61
Pork and shrimp toasts, 51
Prosciutto-fruit bundles, 98
Puff pastry anchovies, 118
Puff pastry croûtes, 150

Quail-egg flowers, 82-3
Quails' and gulls' eggs, 119

Rare roast beef and pickle kabobs, 121

Steak tartare, 55
Strawberry tartlets, 151
Stuffed snow peas, 99
Sweet pancakes, 138
Sweet pastry shells, 151

Tabouli bites, 79
Tandoori chicken with cucumber and yogurt dip, 56-7
Taramasalata toasties, 41
Tex-Mex muffins with chili dip, 88-9
Toastie cases, 148
Toasties with pâté and green peppercorns, 48
Tomato, Mozzarella and black olive kabobs, 106
Tortelloni with hot Provençale dip, 80
Tuna toasts, 103

Venison sausages with cranberry sauce, 52

Wafer-thin slices of raw beef with mustard mayonnaise, 60
Walnut and chèvre sablés, 92
Watercress, cream cheese and tomato roulade, 72